How Big? How Strong?
Hurricanes and Earthquakes

by Nia Stein

PEARSON

Scott Foresman

Editorial Offices: Glenview, Illinois • Parsippany, New Jersey • New York, New York
Sales Offices: Needham, Massachusetts • Duluth, Georgia • Glenview, Illinois
Coppell, Texas • Sacramento, California • Mesa, Arizona

hurricane

ocean

Hurricanes and earthquakes are very different from each other. But in some ways they are the same. Hurricanes and earthquakes can both cause a lot of damage and hurt people.

Hurricanes are huge ocean storms. Earthquakes are sudden movements of parts of the earth's surface.

Scientists measure every hurricane and earthquake.

Hard-Hitting Hurricanes

Scientists use wind speed to measure hurricanes. They use something called the Saffir-Simpson Scale. The scale shows the category of a hurricane and the wind speed.

The higher the category number, the stronger the hurricane is. For example, a category 4 hurricane is stronger than a category 3 hurricane. Category 5 is the strongest, most destructive kind of hurricane.

wind speed: how fast the wind blows

The Saffir-Simpson Scale

Type of Hurricane	Wind Speed in miles per hour (mph)
Category 1	74 to 95 mph
Category 2	96 to 110 mph
Category 3	111 to 130 mph
Category 4	131 to 155 mph
Category 5	more than 155 mph

Hurricane Andrew destroyed many buildings.

Hurricane Andrew **roared** across the Atlantic Ocean in 1992. It was one of the worst storms ever in the United States. This Category 4 storm caused more than 25 billion dollars in damage. Andrew did the most damage in Louisiana and Florida.

---

roared: moved with great noise

Four hurricanes slammed into Florida in 2004.

Florida Hurricanes in 2004

Name	Strength	Date
Charley	Category 4	Aug. 13
Frances	Category 2	Sept. 5
Ivan	Category 3	Sept. 16
Jeanne	Category 3	Sept. 25

Florida was a disaster area after four hurricanes in six weeks!

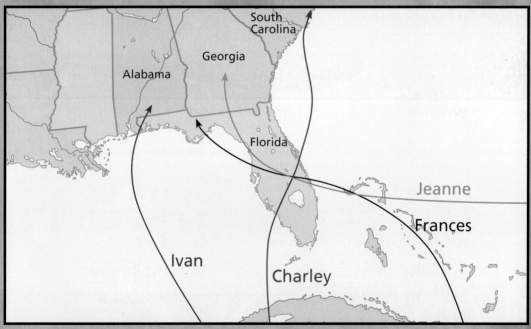

Paths of hurricanes Charley, Frances, Ivan, and Jeanne

slammed into: hit with great force

disaster area: a place of much suffering or loss

Earth-Shaking Earthquakes

An earthquake is a shaking or sliding of the ground. Some earthquakes shake harder than others. Scientists use the Richter (RIK tur) Scale to measure the strength of an earthquake. The numbers on the scale go from 0.0 to 9.0. The highest numbers are for the strongest earthquakes.

Sample of Richter Scale

Number	Damage
Lower than 4.3	Often no damage
4.4 to 4.8	Little damage
4.9 to 5.4	Some damage
6.0 to 6.5	Big damage
6.6 or higher	Major damage

Damage from the earthquake in California in 1994

California has many earthquakes.
An earthquake on January 17, 1994,
awoke many people in the morning. This
earthquake measured 6.7 on the Richter
Scale. It killed 57 people and caused more
than 40 billion dollars in damage.

Damage from the earthquake in Alaska in 1964

The largest earthquake in the United States happened in Alaska in 1964. It measured 8.6 on the Richter Scale.

The largest recorded earthquake in the world struck the country of Chile in 1960. It measured 9.5, and it killed more than 6,000 people.

More than a million earthquakes occur each year. Here's some good news: most are so small, no one even feels them!